Reflections on Fly Fishing

Streamside Notes from Colorado Waters

Photos & Words by Bob Stovern

Bob Stovern
P.O. Box 1063
Paonia, CO 81428

Ordering information:
Special discounts are available on quantity purchases. For details, visit the website below.
www.ReflectionsOnFlyFishing.com

Second Edition, July 2016

ISBN 978-1502898548

Dedicated to all of the creeks, lakes, ponds, streams
and rivers in Colorado.

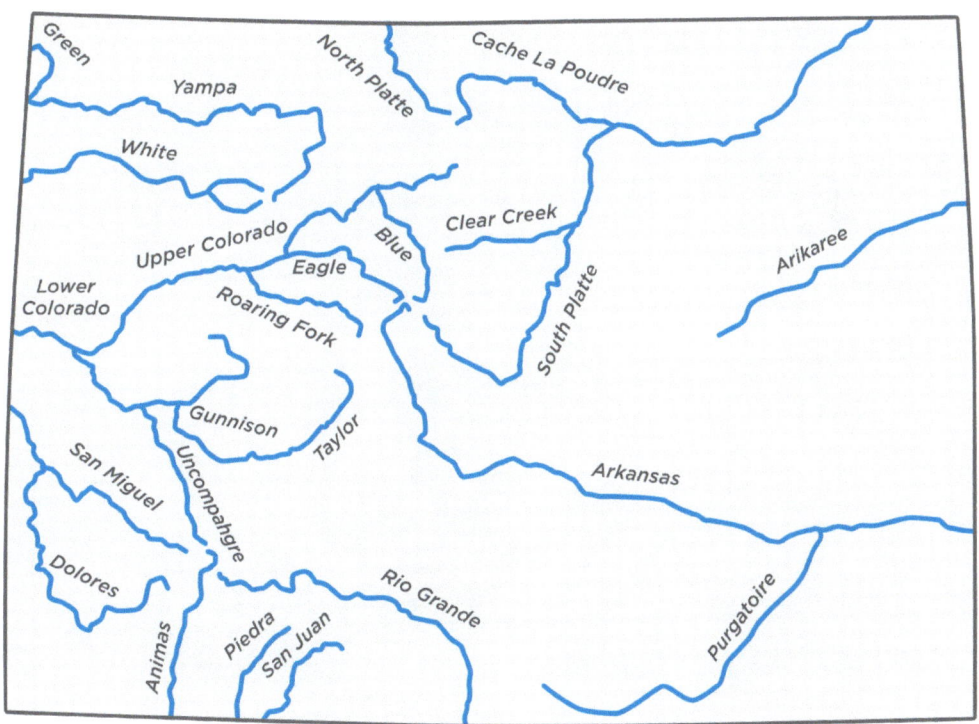

Major rivers originate in the Rocky Mountains of Colorado.

TABLE OF CONTENTS

A fiery red sunrise lights up the Frying Pan River near the tailwater area. ➤

"I wonder what my fish friends are doing today."

Exceptionally clear water on this day in the Animas River near Durango.
Fall fishing in the Gunnison Gorge is spectacular. ➤

Introduction

Even people who don't fly fish dream about it: A solitary figure standing waist deep in water as long loops of line flash gracefully overhead in the warm rays of early sun. Fly fishermen stand out from other fishermen by our unique gear and slow, methodical approach. We disguise tiny hooks as bugs to attract the unsuspecting bite of a naturally feeding fish. While others stop at the water's edge, we step in. In this book, you will find photographs and thoughts gathered from ten years of fly fishing throughout Colorado. Step into your waders and follow me...

Early morning on the Taylor River upstream of Almont, Colorado.
Animas River brown caught and released on my birthday. ➤

1 SHOW UP

The first step to all worthy endeavors. It could be hot out there. The water might be too cold. The day might be too windy or it might be just right. How do you know? The time for guessing is over. Pull on your boots and join the other creatures under the sun. Pass your hands through the grass, let the hair on the back of your neck tell you the direction of the wind and test the water temperature with your fingertips. Flip over a few rocks and see who else is here. Now you know the conditions.

Hand tied nymph pattern attached with open loop knot.
Early light hitting the Arkansas River downstream of Granite, Colorado. ➤

2 GEAR

Planning is the key to success. You are purposely entering this new and unfamiliar environment. You need to be comfortable, but do not burden this short journey today with too many belongings. Decide which tools work best to navigate this foreign terrain before you begin. Step lightly and feel your way along the river bottom. Seek allies as you travel along.

A warm September day on the Animas River was best experienced barefoot.
Friends at a fishing hole in the Black Canyon of the Gunnison. ➤

3 VISION

Sight occupies a significant portion of our brain – but vision is much larger. Vision allows us to see through the cloudiest water and the darkest night. Utilize all five senses to create a full picture. When you find the edges, use your intuition and imagination to paint more details on the canvas. Believe in your quest and "see" through any obstacles. We are very close. The path is clear and the time is near. This is vision.

On a hot day, Hermosa Creek can yield excellent summer fly fishing conditions.
Naturally feeding cutthroat trout in the clear waters of Emerald Lake. ➤

4 LUCK

Follow signs, hear messages and be open to all possibilities. Luck doesn't always have to happen by accident. We position ourselves at every moment, so use these precious seconds wisely. Small adjustments to your presentation defines the difference between sudden success and prolonged solitude. Explore probability. You often receive prizes.

Larger than average cutbow caught and quickly released into the Animas River.
Spring fishing for wary brown trout in the Animas River. ➤

5 KNOTS & SNAGS

Inevitable. Debilitating. Disheartening. A perfect moment has collapsed and forward progress has come to an abrupt halt. Do not fight it. Move gently and deliberately towards the problem. Take advantage of this down time to observe your surroundings. Can you see why this happened? What steps will you take to avoid this obstacle in the near future? New possibilities often reveal themselves during the pause.

Caddis larvae found in the box canyons of the Piedra River near Pagos Springs.
Late sun illuminates the light green waters of the Animas River. ➤

6 WIND

Hello, friend! I know you are my friend because you are always a constant companion - right in front of me or right behind. You blow my hat to one side for the chase, then put grit in my teeth for a taste. Sometimes you whisper encouragement to go forward and other times you howl the clear message to retreat. I politely greet you by name and curse you the same. Listen to the wind.

Full color rainbow trout caught in Emerald Lake with dry fly.
The altitude of Emerald Lake in the Weminuche Wilderness is 10,033 feet. ➤

7 RAIN

Water grows legs and finds a new home. Thunderclouds open and the rain falls right on your head today. Be patient. The storms were distant on the horizon this morning and they will pass soon. The rain stops. This sudden deluge has brought new life to the landscape. Now, we dance!

Post-rain blue winged olive hatch along the Upper Colorado River.
Thunderstorm on the Colorado River with Boulder Boat Works and the train. ➤

8 HIGH WATER

You are not the only one with big ideas. The river has a few of these too. Familiar waters have become so turbulent and confused that you do not recognize them. Keep your belt tight and never take chances here. See the potential dangers of an enormous shifting world that temporarily confronts your path. Offer assistance to others that may not respect this as quickly.

Observing the tea stained white water of the Taylor River during high flows.
The Gunnison River peaked at +9,000 cfs through the gorge in June 2014. ➤

9 THE HATCH

Air, land and water explode with insects. They swarm your line, crawl up your arms and fly into your mouth. The birds, snakes and fish eat them, but we spit them out. Hold your breath and try to blend in. Scan the water as you move and you will see the feeding trout. A hatch happens daily and if you return to the same waters often you will appreciate a larger cycle. The biggest events only happen a few special days each year and some years are better than others. Celebrate the hatch.

Large salomnflies and mayflies can be found sharing the same rock.
Animas River caddis hatches often peak during the first two weeks of June. ➤

10 MOVE ON

There is always a corner around the next corner. Go ahead and take a look for yourself. The world seems to be constructed from corners connected by infinite paths. Vertical and horizontal, zig and zag, up and down, around and through. Some days are for one place while other days are for the next place. Choose your route swiftly to maximize water time. Do not hesitate to alter your path as the journey unfolds before you.

The Gunnison River as it winds its way slowly through the gorge at Ute Park.
The altitude at Dollar Lake near Kebler Pass is close to 10,000 feet. ➤

11 SCHOOLS

A school is more than two moving in the same direction. All of us do it. It can be formally structured or spontaneously wild. If you are fluidly schooling, you are rapidly sharing your knowledge and listening intently as others do this too. We are all in the same water together. Be lucid and candid with collective wisdom and experience. Share the water with others.

Floating the Gunnison River downstream from Black Canyon.
Hatcheries can be a great place to take a break and watch fish behavior. ➤

12 THE BIG ONE

It often gets away, but not always. Allowing your line to go slack and your eyes to wander is a sure way to miss that once in a lifetime opportunity. Be ready at all moments for a strike. Every cast holds the possibility for a sudden positive outcome. Did you know that the big one searches for you just as you search for it? Let yourself be found. Expect success.

Fat brown trout taken on a #4 salmonfly dry pattern in the Gunnison River. +20 inch brown trout caught and released in the Animas River. ➤

13 RELEASE

In the moment is where the real magic happens. Everything before and after this is just a story. Did you know it is possible to catch the same fish more than once? Extend the exhilarating moment of discovery with a subsequent release. Respect your opponent and treat them well, so you both return another day. Practice this often. Congratulations! You have become part of something much bigger than you.

Gently releasing a nice brown trout back into the Upper Gunnison River
Solitude can often be found by hiking the inner trails of the Gunnison Gorge ➤

14 DREAM

You know the day has been a good one when it's over before you know it. What have you been doing for the past seven hours? Where did you go? Consider this the best possible result! The mystery has fully embraced you. If you are thinking about it, you are probably not presently experiencing it. Immerse yourself into the dream and enjoy the ride. There isn't a stopwatch, scoreboard or trophy for finishing first here.

Side channel of the Animas River near the high bridge in Durango, Colorado. In-camera blur of colorful rainbow trout while fishing South Boulder Creek. ➤

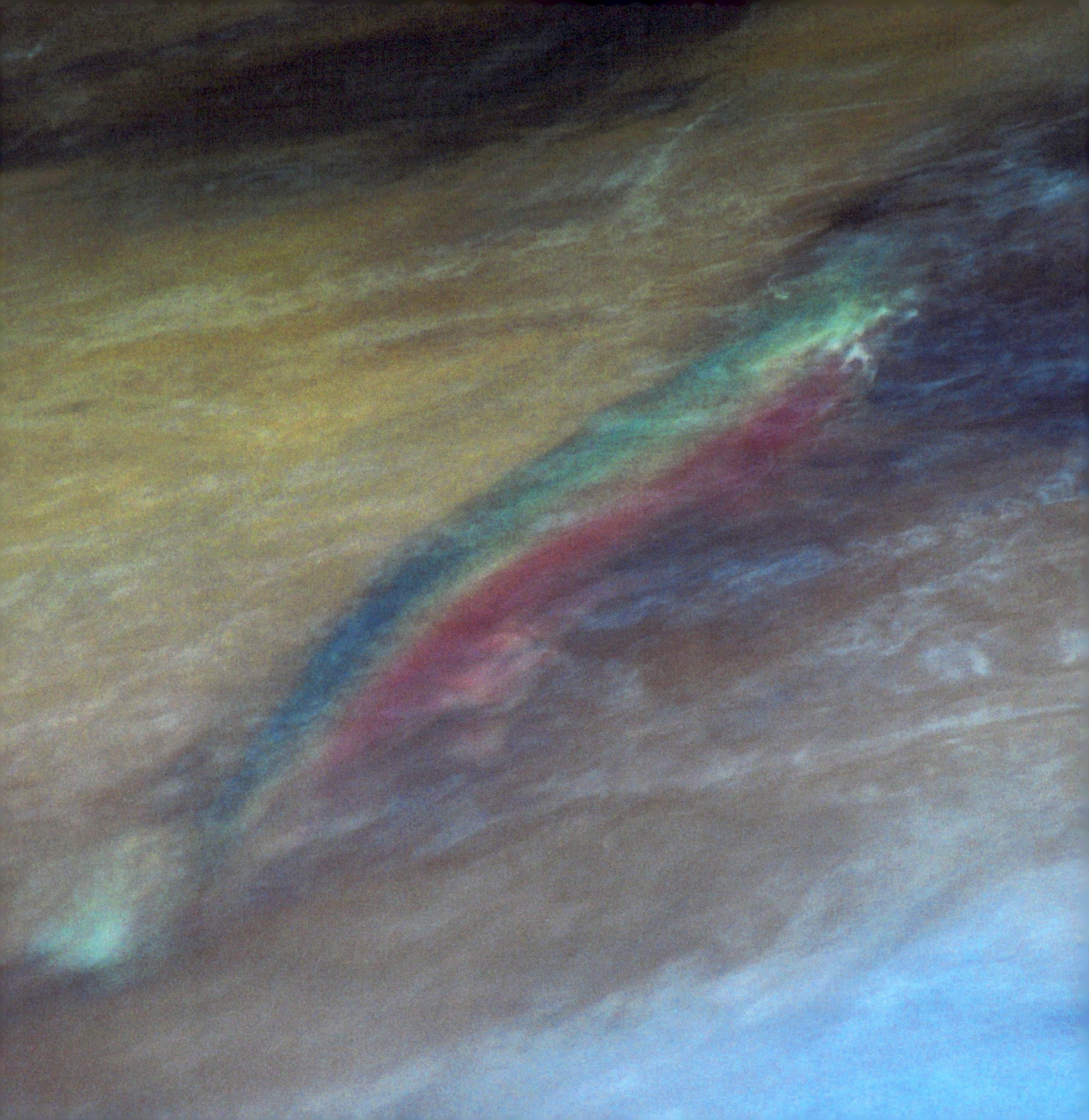

Photography Notes

Cover Photo - Fall fishing in the Gunnison Gorge, October 2009.

Page 1 - Lower Hermosa Creek north of Durango, Colorado, August 2007.

Page 3 - Illustration showing major rivers originating in the state of Colorado.

Page 5 - A fiery red sunrise lights up the Frying Pan River tailwater, September 2006.

Page 6 - Exceptionally clear water day in the Animas River near Durango, July 2007.

Page 7 - (see cover photo notes)

Page 8 - Early morning on the Taylor River near Almont, Colorado, September 2013.

Page 9 - Animas River brown trout caught and released on my birthday, July 2007.

Page 10 - Hand tied nymph attached with open loop knot, November 2006.

Page 11 - Early light hitting the Arkansas River near Granite, Colorado, August 2013.

Page 12 - A warm September day on the Animas River was best experienced barefoot.

Page 13 - Fishing the East Portal in the Black Canyon of the Gunnison, August 2011.

Page 14 - Hermosa Creek can yield excellent summer fly fishing conditions, June 2006.

Page 15 - Naturally feeding trout in the clear waters of Emerald Lake, August 2009.

Page 16 - Large cutbow caught and released in the Animas River, March 2007.

Page 17 - Spring fishing for brown trout in the Animas River, April 2006.

Page 18 - Caddis larvae found in the box canyons of the Piedra River, August 2007.

Page 19 - Late sun illuminates the green waters of the Animas River, September 2006.

Page 20 - Full color rainbow trout caught in Emerald Lake, July 2007.

Page 21 - Emerald Lake is at 10,033 feet in the Weminuche Wilderness, August 2009.

Page 22 - Post-rain hatch along the Upper Colorado River, September 2006.

Page 23 - Thunderstorm on the Colorado River with Boulder Boat Works and the train.

Page 24 - Observing the tea stained white water of the Taylor River, June 2015.

Page 25 - The Gunnison River peaked at +9,000 cfs through the gorge in June 2014.

Page 26 - Stoneflies and mayflies can be found sharing the same rock, June 2010.

Page 27 - Epic Animas River caddis hatch during the first two weeks of June 2007.

Finding healthy trout in crystal clear waters of the Animas River.

About the Author

Bob Stovern is a freelance graphic designer and professional photographer currently living in Paonia, Colorado. He has been a full time resident and avid fly fisherman in Colorado since 1995 and became a dedicated fisherman after landing a 72 pound king salmon as a teenager growing up in Alaska.

Reflections on Fly Fishing is a selection of photographs matched with short essays gathered during ten good years of fly fishing in Colorado creeks, lakes, ponds, streams and rivers. You can see prints of all the images shown in this book and view more of Bob's photography at: **www.BobStovern.com**

For personal correspondence, trip photography or guide recommendations, send email to: bob@bobstovern.com (include subject and contact information).

Bob Stovern fly fishing the Gunnison River (photo by Dana Stovern).

www.ingramcontent.com/pod-product-compliance
Lightning Source LLC
Chambersburg PA
CBHW041525280526
45792CB00004B/1384